THE FLAME

THE FLAME

EANE WATSON

Eane Watson

The Flame

THE FLAME

It breathes, burning
This living thing
Of heat and of light
Brighter, and hotter
Incandescent, pure
Consuming my all
Yet giving me life

DEPARTING

Soon, like a deer
Will she leap, spring
Fleetly away
And I will be left
Suddenly silent
Alone in this glade

OF DREAMS, SHADOWED

Of dreams, shadowed
Dimly recalled, and then
Forgotten, fading
Dissipating as smoke
In cold winds of day

DESCENDING WINTER

No promise, or hope, is held
In these darkening skies
Of warmth, light, or life
Chilling, the wind, the rains
Bleaching all the colour
As day bleeds out to night

AGES INTO AEONS

In the furnace, the forge
Of sleep, dream, and waking
Heartbeats and hammer-strokes
Forging, shaping anew
Continuous and endless
Through life, death, life
Ages into aeons, beyond
Until dust, dross remade
Brighter than the stars

CAN ≠ SHOULD

To freedom, and freedoms
In one thing, or all
We have within our grasp
Yet, despite our petulance
Arguments, opined clumsy
The rights to freedom, freedoms
In all things, or one
Remain unearned, undeserved
And vandals, we are, in Eden

LIGHT FLEES THE VALLEY

Light flees the valley
Beyond westward hills
The sun, and its warmth
Never did reign here
Nor the day hold sway
Light flees the valley
Mocking now, the cold
Spirits, delighting
In whisperings cruel
As mists wreathe and writhe
Light flees the valley
And with it, flies hope
What now, in darkness
Beneath trees, in hearts
Until morning comes

KNOWLEDGE

What is faith but trust, blind
Better, now, certainty
In knowledge
Then pitfalls of belief

MIRROR

Still, I am yet to see
The beauty in all things
Or then, that nothing
Is, is not, beautiful
And that then, then
Perfection of all
The mirror of the skies

WANDERING UNLOST

The air, curling
Through hair golden
Warmed under skies
Blue, and brazen
This shining one
Wandering unlost
In hill glades cool
Shadowed, pale hills
Stilled by the winter

BOUQUET

I can't find any flowers
Worthy enough of you
That are anywhere near
As breathtaking
So, what chance do I have
Then of finding words

SHORES

I find myself on the shores
Having been tossed and thrown
By the tumultuous winds, waves
Of unkind, unquiet slumber
Threatening, darkening clouds
Of nightmare-seed, lowering
Until sea and sky are one
Yet here, you, on these shores
Burning sun-bright and warm
A vision, of everything
That is beautiful and true
Of limb, countenance, grace
Almost too lovely to endure
And I am filled, overflowing
Aching with this love

SUNRISE

Slow turns the hand of time
Until all the world is paused
Heart and breath stills
Waiting, poised expectant
For the sunrise of your return

WINDING

Then, came the wind
Pushing, laughing
Rushing northwards
From frozen seas
The candle trembles
In boisterous draughts
As outside, trees
Sway in wild dance

ON THE SPOT

Nothing comes to mind
When asked for impromptu verse
Realisation blooms

ESSENCE

I can see beneath
The surfaces of you
And then, what is left
When all crumbles, falls
Into dust and shadow
Then the essence true
The aether and the spirit
Children born of fire
As embers escaping
The crucible of the stars
Bright into the void

LATE AUTUMN DAWN

Slowly, softly, comes the morn
Grey-clad, and shrouded hues
The sun distant and dim
Above the mist-wreathed world
And then, uncertain birdsong
Quietly heralds the day

INCALESCENT

Effortless, she is
Shining radiant
Sunlit from within
A summer deity
Harvest-warm smiles
The deep blue skies
Of her heart, mind
Eternal, endless

THE OCEAN ETERNAL

In a moment, soon, I die
An ephemeral current
In the ocean eternal
My truth, and memories
Fading, forgotten, until
Perhaps they never were
By chance, I may return
A ripple upon the sea
Again, again, unending
Or to oblivion, I sink
I do not, cannot, know
But here, now, this
Every thought, action, deed
Matters, means, is
In a moment, now, I live

A FLOWER, CUT

Not uncaring, nor unkind
The blade-wielding hand
Gentle, the razor kiss
Of steel, sap, and stem
A single leaf, falling
Floating to the floor

PERFECT

As summer cools and fades
Autumn breathing, sighs
Tumultuous fever-nights
Dimming into memory
The changing of the days
Anew, what already was
All, one endless moment
Perfect, eternal

HEART(H)

Sunlight fading to rain
Cloud-shadowed, the land
From a distant somewhere
A lonely birdsong comes
Reminding me of the hours
Until I turn for home
Returning then to you
To where my heart is still

VIRUS

It's you, mainly
That I miss, you
Your touch, touching
Skin soft, silken, cool
Beneath my fevered hands
I yearn to surface
From beneath this sea
It's you that I miss
And your, our, love

CABARITA

Sunshine-squalls, dimming
Darkening to rain
Seafoam on slate seas
Flung by the winds
To fall, once again
Like snow on the cove
We went to seek the sun
But as rivers rose
And as skies closed in
You, I found, again

THE VALLEY DIM

Below, the valley dim
In silence, awaiting
Beneath muted trees lie
Pathless, darkened glades
Forgotten, and forgetting
Of men, 'ere my passage
Long lie here the shadows
Of heart, and of days
Yet downward leads my road
Into the quiet unlight
Awaiting, in silence
The valley dim below

A CLOCK WINDING SLOW

With feet, and heart
As heavy as the other
Do I this hill climb
Away from your door
The haven, harbour
Where still you slumber
In peace, beautiful
Until these slow hours
To memory, recede
And then may I return

SHIFTS

The hours awake, drifting
On maples seas of sleep
The skies, unfamiliar
Turning, into darkness
Reaching to hold nothing
Where I dreamt you would be
The days, nights, mere hours
Yet an aeon seeming
Without you here with me

MANIFEST

I stood above it all
The world distant below
To my right, the essence
Everything I should be
Ascending now the stairs
Now, standing between us
The judge, weighing
Now, the scales move

A FLARE, IN UNSEEING EYE REFLECTED

I have seen the end
The ships and their captains
That have, perhaps, sailed
Too far, or not far enough
And are now becalmed
Bewildered, and lost
In waters unfamiliar
The depths awaiting
Fading, and slipping,
Into endless sleep

EAGLE TERRACE

The waves summer-green
Breathing below me
Seen through slender limbs
Of fragrant eucalypts
As the subtle skies
Darken, and lighten
Portents, promises
Of the day to come

KNOWLEDGE

I know nothing at all
This much I know
So, I listen, watch, observe
Remaining in silence
Yet the more that I know
This much I know
I know nothing at all

NEVER LEFT

There is no distance
No time, nor space
Though you are gone
Still, yet, you linger
Empty rooms filled by you
Gone, but never left
There, also here
I will remain
Until you I breathe
Over and again

NIGHT, INTO DAY

I have no memory
Of waking, 'ere the dawn
But clear, do I recall
The rain drifting slow
From sullen skies
Dissolving slow the dreams
Of dying, over and again
Fall, and stand, and fall

A FRAGRANCE, CAUGHT

Even in summer
That half-space, dream
The moments between
Life, death, life
I find her still
Pervading my being
A love that is
Chosen, unchosen
A fragrance caught
Imbuing memory
Of what is yet to come

AESTAS

This goddess of summer
By her am I renewed
My barren wasteland heart
Now with flowers adorned
My soul's forgotten cup
Filled, overflowing

POVERTY

The gold, slipping
Falling through fingers
Wreathing into smoke
A desert mirage, deceiving
Dragons, we become
Hoarding, pursuing
That which never was

TESTS

Searching the night for solutions
Indifferent darkness, silence
The dawn bringing nothing
But subdued, sombre grey
Sunlight – if you can call it that
Replacing the empty night
With hollowness of day
The Gods, silent, watch

HUNTING

Again, I dreamed the dream
The endless miles passing
Summer sun warming
Skies filling heart and lungs
Empty is my mind
Racing on limbs four
Towards the horizons
Seeking the beyond

RETIREMENT HOME

Tepid, the air, atmosphere
These muted pastel walls
Television unceasing
Muzak looping, galling
The lives, stories, tales
Of trapped, lost, souls
Trapped, ignored, futiled
As minds, spirits, hearts
Fade, dissolve to nothing
As if they never were
I would sooner open veins
Than to such death, hell
Be consigned, condemned

APART

Stirring, adrift
On dreamless waters
My hands reaching
Through silences, voids
To find you not
Again, slipping, fading
Beneath the surface
The night-sea breathes

THE UNDYING

Guided am I by Gods
Yet worshipping of none
Clutch and grasp as you will
Your relics and baubles
Mores and superstitions
As you, of I, decry
It takes a heretic
To accuse heresy
Of sin and blasphemy
The wages are the same
What I seek is beyond
Where the light, dark, end
And all is then become

AETHERIAN

From the north, far
Hyperborean plains
In her wake, her coming
Airs of spring, scented, warm
The flowers blossoming
Beneath her dancing feet
Her sorrows, they sear me
The rains washing gently
And yet, even from afar
The moonlight of her gaze
Bright, fierce, heart-sun
Flooding through all I am
Blessed am I by her love
And in my love, returned

HOLD

I breathed you in
Then, in leaving
Lungs and heart full
As the sea-sky
Pales into dawn
In leaving, full
Of heart, of lung
'Til weary feet
Turning to home
Breathing you again

LOST

How far we have fallen
Much has been unlearned
None more so than this
That the Heroes, Gods
Were never somebody
Something, somewhere, else
We have surrendered
Our divinity, grace
And none recall the way

RAMPART

Ever higher, deeper
Trestle, mortar, stone
Do these walls grow
Before, and above me
Yet, even sunlit-warm
Cold grows the day
Beshadowed I become

COMPLACENCE

Of my laurels, evergreen
A bower, a bed, I wove
There, content, I slumbered
Now all has faded, withered
And winter, hard, has come

A DEPARTING

In the sweetness, warmth
Of your embrace, I tarried
It is you I breathe
Rain, Sudden
Darkening, the skies
Leaves in wind currents swirling
My heart overflows

CRUAIDÍN CATUTCHENN

Poised, in a hand
Equally cold and hard
Lugaid's place, or that
Of his right hand
Do I wish to take
Cut the past clean
This severed wrist
So worthy, ready
Of here, now, then
May I truly be

DRINK

This cup, as it is
Steeped in the well
Of endless waters
Overflowing with life
Bright heart-dew, clear
Sustaining endlessly
That which is all
Knowing not an end
Nor beginning

TODAY

On a day like this
The exuberant airs
Warm, cool, and both
Laughing as it races
Tousling my hair
Beneath a sky, turning
Its eternal face to spring
On a day like this, yes
I could live, die, and live

PRAYER

I asked to be tested
Forged, made pure
Strong, and worthy
Expecting foes, war
Bold adversaries
As equals, to meet
Battles, and threats
To sink teeth into

I asked to be tested
Polished, refined
A mirror clear and bright
I did not expect ghosts
Pitfalls, traps, snares
Knives and whispers
In the dark unseen
And wounds, unhealing

I asked to be tested
So as to stand tall
Among men, the Gods
And thus, I will
For blessed am
To be given, gifted
That which I need
And not what I want

FIELD TRIP

I knew you had gone
Like a bird, flown
Key in lock, I paused
Anticipating the silence
Observations, of things
A pan on the stove
In the vase, flowers
Your perfume, lingering
Voicelessly naming
The absence of you

THE PARTING

With each passing day
And the blossoming
The breaking dawn of us
Do I then mourn keener
Each moment, hour apart
Every kiss goodbye
Even yet knowing
Eternity awaits us
The forever that is ours

VISITOR

The white ships, fair
Have long since sailed
To horizons, west
And then, beyond
Yet I remain here
To learn, toil seek
Until the return
A stranger, am I
Upon these shores

PHOENIX

What is this thing
A fire, burning
Consuming all
Yet breathing life
Flames of many hue
Brilliant heat
Neither smoke, ash
Impurity, remains
Holiness unknown
Outside of heaven
A love, blessed
Sanctified, sacred

WONDER

Lit from within
This fey one
I hold her close
Warm in the night
Subtle, her power
Slender, and strong
A wondrous blade
Wreathed in silk
A queen, ethereal
Here in my arms

FLOWERS

There, in the window
Simply being, breathing
Neither more, nor less
But only, exactly
Their very perfection

IN GREETING

The distant song
Of the bird, unseen
Trembles at edges
Of my hearing
A zephyr cool
Brushed, ripples
My heart-water

UNNEEDED

No one is coming
There is nothing else
No saviour, no God
Cold, the horizon
Breath, have I, and will
Secret Óðr-fire
Victory within
My own God, I am
Saviour-self, am I

A FEW DAYS

The sun rose today
Yet the world has no colour
To the north, heaven
That Door Beyond
Death consumes me
The greatest of trials
That door beyond
Pervades my very being
To live, to die, to live
The very thing you fear
That you shun, and name
In superstitioned whisper
I yearn for, and long
Striving to complete
That which must be done
Learned, known, and known
To be worthy of my time
And win the wages due

VENEER

All around, above, below
Surrounding, immersing
Hollow formulations
Structures and patterns
Thin incantations of man
Endlessly recreated
Yet, beyond, beneath
Calling, beckoning

IRRESISTIBLE

Magic deep and wild
Endless, timeless, true
That as, is, shall be
To which I will return

REDOUBT

Beside me, the deer
Pauses, as north-winds
Gently sing, sigh
Quietly, I watch
As her head, heart
Turn this way, and that
Free is she to choose
Quietly, I watch

HYPNOPOMPIA

Something awaits
Eternal, vast
Beyond these reeds
Rustling whispers
As endless skies
Pale into dawn

HOLLOW

I don't know how
It came to this
Emptiness
Sitting on the bench
Homeless, hopeless
The world passes by
How, how, how
Did it come to this

UNALTARED

I saw her there
Before the dawn
The moonlight pale
Though cloud-hidden
From her eye shone the Goddess bright
Of starlit hue
Her mortal raiment
Cannot her conceal
Wreathed as she is
In a light divine
Inner light divine

LOINNIR GHRÉINE

Her returning
Is as sunlight
Breaking clouds
Colour flooding
Wintered earth

LENS

Angels and Gods
We perceive, portray
In our own image
Yet monsters, demons
As something else
Something other
Anything but like us
And what is not us
Something other
Something else
As demons, monsters
Anything but like us

AS SHE WANDERS BY

She of the dawn
Unassuming, unknowing
Her own magic, beauty
As she dances, elfin
In her light and grace
Flowers in hearts bloom
As she wanders by

She of the sun
Unknowing, unassuming
Her goodness, greatness
As she bears starlight
In her heart and eye
Sunlight through darkness flows
As she wanders by

THAW

Embracing winter
Solitude-content
Within my walls
Yet then you came
A joyous sunrise
Heralding spring
In wonder, I find
Doors, windows open
Corridors flooded
In light, warm
And a fire kindled
On the long-cold hearth

36 HOURS

A few precious hours
Between the coming home
And again, the farewell
Yet the time meant naught
Slowed, then stood still
You, and I, and us
Caught, catching, forever
Where summer gives way
Breathing into fall

LYRIDIA

Under stars dimmed
By the city-glow
We watched
As the Lyrids
Argent, urgent
Fireworks silent
Portent flares
Lighting our hearts
Burning the autumn night

COMEDIA

The moment when
I thought I knew
Then realisation
I know nothing
Over and over
Time, time again

BETWEEN AND BOTH

In the winding
Of the hours small
Signs and portents
Messages, messengers
Of realms and Gods
To which, from, doors
Silently opening
Standing on edges
Of shadow and light
Between, and of
Awakening
And the dream

TEMPLES

Shelley, while weaving
His own tapestries
Verses wondrous
Yet lamented
Despairing
At Byron's altar
As do I, ashamed
Before his shrine
My work, unlettered
Unlit, and crude
A vagrant amongst
The lofty and high

WESTWARD

Slivered moon
Suspended
Beyond mountains dim
Mirror-black waters
Its star-salted song
Beckons me to you

HARVEST

What I sow
The wind, reaps
A tempest harvest
Neither good
Nor ill, it be
Drumming rains
And winds fierce
Giving, taking
Destroying, create

GHOST

The departed, in leaving
Never truly gone
Yet sometimes, return
A test, a choice
Of what then
Becomes

VANAWOD

It falls away
The form, mind
Beyond the spirit
Into spirit pure
Clear, clean, the torrent
Coursing through
Drowning with life
The absolute
Until it, and i
Are one

HAVING DESCENDED

Golden, she is
Suns-blessing
In human form
Silver, the glow
Soft moonlight
Of her gaze
It is a wonder
A mystery
That many behold
But few, few
Ever truly see

TAJ MAHAL

It was there
That table
Along the wall
I looked at you
And you, me
A moment
We both saw
And wondered

CLEAR SKY

And the blue sky
Appeared, vibrant
Yet, it was never
Anything but here
For those minds
Unclouded

2 A.M.

In the small hours
Where heart-shadows
Whispering, cajole
No power I give them
Things that dwell
Beneath light's edge
Wreathed in fear, doubt
Unworthy of my glance
These things that lie
And hide from me in shame

CAMDEN HAVEN

Along the river
A mere stream
Now brown, swollen
We wandered
Waters streamed down
Through eucalypt fingers
Green and shadowed
Dim-remembered
Paths of distant youth
Where still dwells
Innocence

UPSALL'S CREEK

South, beyond
Thew river cold
Hills rising solemn
Tree-spears pierce
Mist-wraiths
Silent, and slow
Falls the rain
In, I breathe
These fields, home
I may never
Know again

HIGHWAY

We crested the ridge
Before us, plains
Green rolling
To cloud-browed
Mountains grey
Onwards, and on
We travelled
You, I, us

WELL

Up, it swelled
Bubbling
This laughter
As a spring
Flowing over

PAUSE

We struggle, die
Climbing this mountain
Straining, upwards
For the heavens
When, we are
Now, and ever
Already the earth
And the skies

THE ROOM

This door, long ago
Did I lock and bar
Against what, and why
I remember not
The window, cracked
Offers little more
Than glimpses, fragments
Of childhood memory
This door, long have I
Shunned its shadow
Against what, and why
I do not know
The whispers, troubled
Grow, clamour louder
My hand, paused
On the handle

A RIPPLE ON THE POND

If, for a moment
We were still
Would we know
With all senses
The deep, vast

MAGIC OF ALL

The very essence
Of existence
Our own true nature
The ripple becoming
Still waters
Once again

INFINITE

As the mayfly
Knows a lifetime
From the morn
Unto the dusk
Summers, winters turn
Circles spinning
Within circles
Galaxies in atoms
The sun merely
An electron's arc

1,000 METRES

Halfway there
She smiled
Gliding away
Down the lane
Effortless
Through the water
Labouring
I followed

STRANGER

You look like
Someone
That I know
Those eyes, unlit walls
Against what, perhaps who?
I cannot know the things
That brought you here
To this place, condition
Yet, you look like
Someone
That I know

THE FIRST STORM OF AUTUMN

Rifle-shot thunder
A fusillade becoming
Underwater, breathe

NIGHT, INTO DAY

Sand-grain eyes, smoke-stung
Sleep beckons, whispers
Sweet temptations
Yet duty cold, hard
Is my God

DESTINY

From the west, they called you
Beyond the setting sun
To a dream, long held
My breath, held
As you choose

THE CLOUD, RED

There, it lives
Beneath the skin
Waiting, the summons
By breath, and by will
The furious cold
Hard, clear ice
A madness-not
This freeing of bonds
Loosing of fetters
This blessing, curse
Of the Father
Gladly, will I bear

CENEL'S ISLAND

Without limit, nor end
Unconditioned
Immovable, irresistible
Yet, by so many
Unseen, unknown
Unimagined, this
Great, wondrous music
Unheard through
Hands, over ears

IN A MOMENT, EONS

Above the earth
Beneath skies
In all directions
Horizons seen, unseen
There, and here
Am I one
Nothing, and yet
Everything

NOT DROWNING

This sea, unfathomed
Its currents deep
Broad upon the water
And below, beneath
I breathe in

THE RACE

The faster we run
I cannot catch you
Nor can you, me
Let's slow down
The air breathe
And be here

UNQUIET

Her fingers stained, tremble
As the cigarette
Smouldering
Smoke-wreathed
Slow-burning
Falling, into ashes

BRIDGES

The pale sky above
Cool earths below
And I am here
In this world, of the other
And somewhere in between
Dawn, and the Day
A dream, it was
Yet you, me
The horizons
Escaping into us

CHOICE

A woman, I found
Human, yet divine
Of light, and peace
Beautiful, within as without
To love her, a choice
And no choice at all
A woman, I found
Divine, yet human
And somehow
Some wonderful how
She chose me in return

TIME AND SPACE

Thoughtlessness
Error, folly, a wound
Given to you, and to me
My intentions matter not
It cannot be undone
So, here then I sit
Without answers
Atonements eluding
I wait, hope, pray
To silent Gods
That you return

SACROSANCT

Breath, and will
Gifted already
By Gods upon me
Thus, then I ask
For nothing – no prayer
Shall I utter, beseeching
At no altar, I worship
My toil and deeds
These gifts, applied
Unaided, alone
Shall my religion be
Here, and now
My heaven

RIGHT SWIPE

I was content to be alone
And, then, you...
You, dangerous at first sight
Everything, a woman should be
In my heart, eyes, mind
Intelligent, courageous
Inquisitive and aware
And now, here we are
There is nothing
No life, or breath
Without you

SOWILO

The rune-cast again
Yet spake of the same
From crisis and strife
A journey alone, and
Awakening
To knowledge, wisdom divine
To walk beyond, higher
As one with the Gods
Should, this I choose to be
That few can, will, want
To walk with me

NO DISTANCE

Somewhere between waking
And the dreaming
Your lips brushed mine
As gossamer
I awoke, and you
Distant miles from here
Yet here...
So very here

IN THE WOODS

I walked away from the fire
Into the dark, among trees
Alone, under myriad stars
Embracing, the fullness
Emptiness of the night

APART

Night falls, and with it
My spirit, mind wander
To you, far
Yet so near

BRIGHT STAR

Long have I toiled, tarried
In the night and shadow
Until you, Bright Star
My heart in your hand
Walked with me
Into the dawn

PAUSE

Minutes roll into hours
Inexorable
Yet, then time
With you and us
This moment only
And forever, endless
Without horizon

THE ARCHER

What then can be said
Of you, of I, of us
Words, shot as arrows
Into the sky, falling
Failing to touch heaven
In futile hope, vain
Still, I draw, release
Again, and again

LIMITLESS

Among stars, shall we walk
Unfettered by time
Nor the horizon

GONE

I know you're still here
But my words spoken'
And unspoken, fall
Into the silence
Turning, looking for you
Knowing full well
You're no longer here
Echoes, fragrances
Of you haunt me

LETTERS

I awoke
In awe
Wonder
Of us
And what
Is yet
To come

ASCENT

Below limb, leaf and bough
Through wind, unfettered
Offering myself to Gods, wild
Thus descends, falls, rains
I am still, silent
Sacrifice
Offerings, myself
All that I am
I give, and lose
Yet then find
Thus, am I renewed
Darkness, lifting
And now, bright
Comes the dawn
Your light within me
Mine burning within you
Ignites, heralds
Rises the sun

INDIA

I remember well that moment
Beholding you in wonder
This heavenly thing before me
Knowing I was but one, ordinary
And you, extraordinary
One who could, can
Have anyone, anything
Praying, hoping
It would be me

HEARTHS

I could not
Imagine
Anything
Anyone
But you
And us

THE HUNT

The words elude me
I pursue them set snares
Yet I return, again
With empty hands
And unfilled pages
Unable to tell, write, of her
That light within
Behind her eyes
Her lengths, curves
Deer-grace, dancing
Across the room
And that smile
Oh, that smile

DRAM

It is a night
To take pause
Crystal. Ice
And fires
Of Islay

OF LOVE

This tale, would I tell
This picture, painted
Of the vast, limitless
Two souls, journeys
Side by side
Without end

SPM

Unsimple
This magnetism
I am drawn
Stronger
In spite
Of the miles

SORROW

Subtle things, the doubts
These hesitations
The wound deep, and scars
On your precious heart
These things grieve me
The hurts
I yearn to heal

THREE NIGHTS

I awoke alone
To silence
Without, within
Waiting for the sun
Stars, and heavens

COUNTRY

A thousand miles
Ten nights, days
Counting down
Distance and time
Waiting with nought
But this moment
Gossamer is the wind

ABOVE, YET BELOW

Standing, sunlit, yet wreathed
Self-shadowed
Eschewing the rose
For thorn-grip flagellation
Bearing of wounds
Whether self-wrought
Or life's barbs driven deep
What madness, to drown
Oneself in the mire
Poetry, the wine
Songs of the Gods
Yet this, this
The suffering
Incoherence of fools

MOMENT

Time, space, distance
None exist, all dissolve
When thinking of you

WEST

With the dawn
Came the wind
Cleansing the day
Sunlight washing over
Hearts, and hands held close
As horizons await her

YOU I NEED

It used to be
A desire, a want
But now, as
The sun, sky
Oxygen

AUGUST ENDING

We awoke to the wind
Cool, yet it bore
Traces, scents, of summer

BRIGHT

The mountain-cloud
Shades, lights
Shining
As heavens
Swirl above

TINÚVIEL

Her kisses
Sweet as wine
Nightingale song

CAFÉ BREAKFAST

Sitting together
Faces, expressions
His, hers
I cannot read
Yet, a sense
Sadness quiet
A distance
Sitting together
Or, perhaps
Apart

A CONSTANT

Waters rise, quickening
The winds buffeting
Restless, the season
Gather your cloak
And be still
Waves are not the ocean
Skies beyond clouds

MEMORIAM

I care not
That my name
Should be known
Remembered by man
Alone I shall stand
And, thus, fall
Let the Gods
Bear witness
And remember

FIRST LIGHT

I awoke
Pre-dawn light
Warm skin on mine
The scent, fragrance
Of her hair
Nothing
Else was
Imbue
My words are
My words
No more, less
I light the candle
Of memory
And thought
Why then hunt
For shadows?

BEECHMONT

Smoke-scent lingering
Mountain-hue and winter sun
In the stillness, love
Opening
Of limits, we speak, conditions
On the unconditioned
And the limitless
As those cowering, trembling
Beneath endless skies
Before vast horizons

SUNSET

Embers of the day
Glow on horizons
The fire burns low
To be rekiundled
Come the dawn

SLOW BURN

Your ashes of doubt
Smoulder, smoke
Burning you
As well as me
I do not ask
To quell them
Let's you and I
Build, stoke
A hotter, brighter
Different flame

WEEKEND

In the sunlight and air
When the world falls away
There is nothing
Except love
Heart-drums, and breath

CAST

Falling, the shards
Into the circle
Algiz, Othala, Wunjo
Near and far
Together, apart
This, I ponder
No questions I ask

IT GROWS

Time, and again
My heart
In your hands
Yours in mine
And nothing else
Existing

OPENING

I have for you
No words
Only the songs
Of my heart

FULL MOON

Smoke curls from chimneys
The sky pales to night
Streets fading, dark
As vision turns within
Beneath quiet, lunar strains
A few lines of nothing
Etched onto a page

ACT

I would rather
Deeds over words
In labour, in battle
Life, and in love

A TORN PAGE

The paper's edge
Rough, uneven
Speaks to me
Of hair warm
And a smile

NORTHBROOK

Together we walk
Greet the tree, living
Towering ancient
Sun-mottled green
A mountain's silence
And there is naught
But you, I, us

ALIVE

Under a dappled sky
Among murmuring trees
Upon the breathing earth
I live, I love, I am

QUARTER, ONE AND ONE

It's been three months
A week, and a day
And I've been mute
As Beren, struck dumb
Amidst Doriath's hills
And the pen, the songs
Have in fallow lain
The words blooming
In my heart

TORRENTS

This river rises
In silent flood
Washes through
Drenching
My very soul

AIR, WATER

I breathe you
Drink you in
And that
Is everything

JINX

I've hesitated
Held back from
These words
Lest I am woken
From this dream
Windchime
Wind through
Bamboo chimes
Outside the window
Staccato sound
Music of peace

www.ingramcontent.com/pod-product-compliance
Lightning Source LLC
Chambersburg PA
CBHW050315010526
44107CB00055B/2248